M000304880

100 Ways To Be
More Like Your Cat

To Shawnie and
Chris

100 Ways To Be
More Like Your Cat

Feline Wisdom for Happy Humans

Celia Haddon

Shaw nie knows
how to live!

yellow
kite

To Paul Rose

First published in Great Britain in 2018 by Yellow Kite
An imprint of Hodder & Stoughton
An Hachette UK company

1

A CIP catalogue record for this title is available from the British Library

Hardback ISBN 978 1 473 68187 3
eBook ISBN 978 1 473 68188 0

Typeset in Celeste by Hewer Text UK Ltd, Edinburgh
Printed and bound in Great Britain by Clays Ltd, St Ives plc

Hodder & Stoughton policy is to use papers that are natural, renewable
and recyclable products and made from wood grown in sustainable
forests. The logging and manufacturing processes are expected to
conform to the environmental regulations of the country of origin.

Yellow Kite
Hodder & Stoughton Ltd
Carmelite House
50 Victoria Embankment
London EC4Y 0DZ

www.yellowkitebooks.co.uk

Feline Ways to Live Wisely

1.

Be your true self

Each cat has its own unique purrsonality. Cats are not conformists. They do not worry about what others think about them. They calmly do their own thing. Cats are one of the most successful species in the world. They serenely accept human adoration, sleep on our beds and dine on expensive cat food. It's a good life!

2.

Live in the present moment

Your cat doesn't worry about what might happen tomorrow or regret what happened in the past. He lives in the present minute. Let go of the past and future, and focus your thoughts upon now.

3.

Accept your life as it is

———

Cats may not welcome change, but they are flexible enough to adjust themselves to it. Cats don't do 'If only . . .' or 'What if . . .?' thinking. They understand that it is what it is. Fighting against what cannot be changed is exhausting. Cats are good at saving energy for more rewarding activities.

4.

Be patient

Ever seen your cat waiting at a mouse
hole? Cats can outwait almost every
other living being. If you really want
something, be prepared to wait for it.
Don't insist on instant results.

5.

Be purrsistent

If your cat can't catch a mouse today, he will go back tomorrow to sit outside the mouse hole again. Purrsistence works. If at first he doesn't succeed, he will try and try again. Don't give up too soon.

6.

Know when *to give up*

———

Your cat, like most cats, only purrsists if
she thinks she has a chance of success. If
she knows she hasn't, she will just walk
away. This is why she hasn't bothered to
learn to open the fridge door. It's too
difficult and, besides, she knows you will
open it for her.

7.

Self-pity and whining are not a feline fault

——

Dogs whine when they are unhappy and humans whine when they think life is unfair. Your cat stays silent. Over thousands of years, cats have learned that self-pity is self-defeating. It's better to move on.

8.

See mistakes and failures as an opportunity to learn

——

Trial and error is how your cat learns when he faces a new experience. Mistakes are the way to learn what *not* to do. The trial-and-error method works for humans as well as cats. So don't let mistakes or failures make you anxious or unhappy. Use them to do better next time.

9.

Be aware

——

Your cat monitors herself and her
territory all the time. That is how she
notices if a bit of chicken falls to the
kitchen floor or if a small crumb has
fallen behind the armchair. If you live
blindly, you miss so much. Your indoor
cat will check out the door to the food
cupboard several times a day, waiting for
that moment when you have forgotten to
close it. Never miss a lucky chance.

10.

Be brave about pain or discomfort

———

Cats show fortitude when it comes to aches and pains or even severe wounds. They do not show that they hurt. Arthritis and other ills of old age may affect cats, but unlike humans they do not moan about them. Complaints bore others and cats are never boring.

11.

Don't live according to the expectation of others

——

Cats do not need or want approval. They are never people pleasers, yet we love them all the more for that free spirit. Not everybody likes cats and not everybody will like you. So what!

12.

Above all, retain your dignity

From the scruffiest cat on the street to the prize pedigree feline, cats have an innate dignity that rarely if ever leaves them. In the face of disappointment, danger and even death, feline dignity remains unimpaired.

Feline Ways to Work Wisely

13.

Don't be a workaholic

No cat is, has been, or ever will be a
compulsive worker. Keep a sensible
work–life balance.

14.

Be above status

Cats don't have hierarchies. They may
live with other cats, but there is no
recognised top cat or pack leader. There
are no feline presidents, prime ministers,
CEOs, rock stars, or TV presenters. Your
cat doesn't struggle to get to the highest
branch of a tree, or compete with
neighbouring cats that have found a
better position on the garden wall. Every
cat is confident about its status as a
supreme feline being.

15.

Money isn't everything

———

Your cat doesn't bother with it at all, yet she has everything she needs. She lives without cash, handbags, purses, bank accounts or credit cards, and she has no debts.

16.

Cats don't talk

Learn from them the value of silence and the power of restraint. Don't talk unwisely in the office or the canteen. If in doubt, stay silent.

17.

Cats are never servile or slavish

Strive for emotional detachment from rude bosses or difficult colleagues. Their behaviour may be a problem for you, but you did not cause it and you cannot change it. If you cannot live with it, walk away from the job. Your cat would.

18.

Do one thing at a time

—

Multitasking leads to hurry and worry.
Cats are single-minded in their actions.
Watch your cat while she is hunting a
mouse or just play hunting a toy. Her
whole mind is on the task. She is not
trying to groom herself or eat while she
is doing it. Her mind is fully focused.

19.

Take a break from working on a screen

Draping yourself on the keyboard like your cat does may not be the wisest way of doing this, but you can get up from your chair and stretch! Rest your eyes and rest your mind by looking out of the window. Cats do a lot of window watching. There is a lot to see – skies, sunsets, clouds, moon, stars, city and country landscapes.

20.

Rise above other people's bad behaviour

Cats have purrfected a look of silent disdain for when they don't like what humans are doing. Practise *that* look. Disdainful looks are powerful put-downs when verbal reproaches might be unwise. Silence can be very effective.

21.

Know when to sheath your claws

────

Your cat conceals her claws in a deliciously soft velvet paw. Try pleasantness as a tactic around colleagues. Even if you are not getting on with others at work, be really amiable. When all else fails, fall back on the power of being nice. Cats purr loudly and often when they want you to give them something. It usually works.

22.

Give yourself a little wash and brush-up pause

———

This helps compose yourself when you are under pressure at work. Cats often do a little grooming when they are in perplexity. It restores their serenity.
A short visit to the office toilet will give you a chance to calm down. It reduces stress and allows clear thinking.

23.

Celebrate your successes

Make sure those around you know about your achievements. The gift of a dead mouse to your boss may not be exactly what is required: instead make sure the boss knows about that award, that expertise, that ten thousandth customer or that letter of thanks. Cats are not modest about their hunting success. When they've caught it, they flaunt it.

Feline Ways to
Have Fun

24.

Make time for play

—

Play is an essential part of the good life. Nobody is too old to play. Kittens play, but so do elderly cats. Your cat enjoys playing with you, but when she's feeling happy, she will also play on her own. Play is important for human and feline wellbeing.

25.

Plenty in life is free, according to your cat

He will amuse himself with a feather, a bit of old newspaper, some scrunched-up tinfoil. Amusements for humans don't always need a lot of money either. The streets, the footpaths, the parks, the riversides and the forests are all free for you to enjoy.

26.

Get high in moderation

Cats like catnip, but they don't get addicted to it or spend all day sniffing it. They use it for a few minutes, enjoy the buzz, and then they stop and walk away normally.

27.

Take pleasure in small things

———

Cats go crazy for little toys like furry mice, not large ones like Aston Martin cars or designer handbags. Be like your cat.

28.

Uplift your spirits by climbing high

———

Your cat enjoys tree climbing, fence walking, or just sitting on top of the wardrobe looking down at you. You may be too old to climb trees, but you can still enjoy climbing a hill. Or even a mountain. Being high up in the world is an inspiration.

29.

Go on a nature safari

———

Nature renews the spirit and being close
to nature is good for humans as well as
cats. There are animals and plants all
around us, even in cities. Keep an eye out
for passing cats, dogs and other wildlife.
See if you can spot a cat in the window
of the houses you go past. Look at the
plants growing at the roadside or
pushing through cracks in the concrete.

30.

Whenever you can, walk don't drive

Cats never travel by car, trains or plane, if they can avoid it. Your cat walks slowly and carefully round its territory. Even in a small area, she will walk round it several times a day. So walk – in your street, in the park, on the way to work, in the countryside, or (if all else fails) on a walking machine in the gym. Walking is good for feline and human health.

31.

Take up ornithology as a hobby

Your cat does a lot of bird watching. Even pigeons in a city square are fun to watch – look out for their cooing mating rituals, their winged flight, and the glossy iridescent feathers on their neck. See if you can spot their nests high up on the ledges of buildings. And where there are pigeons, there may be birds of prey to watch too.

32.

Shop for what you need

—

Not for what you want, or what you *think* you want. Shopping is not a feline recreation. Choose joyful experiences rather than more stuff.

33.

Go hunting

———

No need to kill like your cat does. Just go on a photo shoot. Capture nature by camera or video. Your cat is full of pride and satisfaction when she has successfully captured a mouse or a thrown cat toy. Enjoy the human version of her hunting success by posting your photos on your social media site.

34.

Chasing a small ball is fun for a solitary cat

They do not need other players. You can play tennis against a wall, dribble a football round the garden, practise basketball shots, or teach yourself to juggle. There's no need for competition. Just enjoy it on your own.

35·
Go fishing

Fishermen know, as cats know, that actually catching a fish is not the true purpose of fishing. The real pleasure is simply sitting on the bank in the sunlight, doing nothing in particular while *thinking* of catching a fish. Watch your cat sitting by the garden pond doing just that.

Feline Ways to
Make a Home

36.

*Make your house
or flat into a home,
not a show place*

———

Your cat marks her home territory by
rubbing her familiar scent on its
favourite places. Make your territory into
a home by marking it with familiar items
that mean a lot to you. And think about
getting a cat if you haven't already got
one!

37.

Be chilled about furniture and fittings

Your cat doesn't have any stuff. She doesn't bother with the right kind of designer cat bed. A cardboard box may give her more pleasure than the expensive cat item within it. She won't ever need to declutter.

38.

As every cat knows, comfort is more important than style

Soft carpets or rugs and cosy furniture please your feline friend more than noisy bare floors or tiles. A house that isn't comfortable is a display house not a home.

39.
Safe havens

When cats get upset or stressed, they
need a safe haven where they can chill
out until they feel better – maybe under
the bed or on top of the wardrobe.
Humans need safe havens too – it might
be on a bench in the garden, under the
duvet in the bed, inside a church or
temple, in the office cloakroom, or just at
the kitchen table near the warm stove.

40.

Familiar is better than new for a comfortable home

———

Don't be a compulsive purchaser, a crazy spring cleaner, or an obsessive interior redecorator. Cats like a stable familiar environment. A house should be a home, not a design studio or a building site.

Feline Ways to
Eat Well

41.

*Feel free to choose
the more expensive
items on the menu*

———

Your cat would.

42.

Eat your greens

Cats regularly enjoy eating grass. Some also love asparagus and a little broccoli, though a fully vegetarian diet is bad for them.

43.

If you don't care for the food, leave something for Mr Manners

———

Something better might turn up later in the day. Your cat has no compunction about leaving a little food if she chooses, confident you will offer her something better.

44.

Drink enough water

———

A beautiful glass may encourage this. Cats have strong individual preferences for drinking bowls. Plastic or metal tableware is often a turn-off for both cats and humans.

45.

Don't let the weight pile on

———

Most cats that live a natural life never get fat. Many cats learn how to regulate their own intake and will eat only when they are hungry, not when they are greedy.

46.

Eat little and often

—

That's what cats like to do. It is better for the digestion than one gigantic meal a day.

47.

Stay away from too much sugar

It's bad for you. Cats don't have a sweet tooth. So they don't gorge on sweet stuff. So they usually stay slimmer. Avoiding too much sugar will keep you healthier *and* slimmer.

48.

Don't be afraid to eat out

Cats often help themselves to cat food in other people's houses. Why slave over a hot stove when someone else could cook for you?

49.

Regular meals are the healthy way to eat

———

Your cat expects meals to turn up on time and will often remind you about his food. Never eat on the run. It's bad for your digestion.

*Feline Ways to
Care for Others*

50.

Avoid conflict whenever possible

Think of other means of getting your own way. Your cat is good at getting his own way, whether it is food, bed or affection. You could learn from him.

51.

Allow other people to have different opinions

Cats do not have opinions about politics, religion, or philosophy. Or if they do, they keep them secret. Their attitude to others is *Live and Let Live* unless that other is a mouse. Cats do not want your opinions and you do not want theirs. You will never be able to change them and they do not wish to change you. Imitate their serenity and don't get into arguments with others.

52.

Train your family and friends without their knowing

———

You may not have realised it, but your cat has trained you to provide what he wants. Now apply the same training to your human family. Praise (the equivalent of purrs) when they do what you want. Ignore, rather than claw, unwanted behaviour. Punishment doesn't work. It just makes cats and people angry. Reward works better.

53·
Be a good listener

Your cat listens to what you say without interrupting or giving advice.

54.

*Your cat keeps
your secrets and
her own secrets*

———

Keep other people's secrets and keep
your own. Be a trustworthy friend.

55.

Play with your family and friends as much as possible

Let others win sometimes. Ever watched cats play? Cats understand that play has to be reciprocal and uncompetitive. It's not about winning. They know that sometimes they have to self-handicap or lose the game in order to make sure their playmate is enjoying it too.

56.

Charm the birds off the tree

Your cat often charms you into rewarding him with treats and titbits. Charm works better than coercion. Try it more often.

57.

Only sleep with loved ones

———

Otherwise sleep alone.

58.

Gentle touch is the way your cat shows she loves you

She rubs against you. So touch, hug and kiss your friends, but don't do it to strangers. They might not like it, or they might like it too much. Your cat enjoys being petted by you, but she is selective. She doesn't want complete strangers trying to pet her. Learn to respect her and other people's boundaries.

59.

Do not try to possess your partner

Cats enjoy the fun, but they don't insist on a lifelong commitment. Your cat has never demanded a marriage contract, a joint account or a piece of expensive jewellery. They know that a relationship cannot be bought or sold. Give a partner freedom so that love can flourish freely.

60.

If you do or must stray, come back as soon as you can

———

Cats always come home and they never, *ever*, kiss and tell.

61.

Do not be emotionally needy

———

Your cat is not. He can get on with his own life without depending on you emotionally. He will ask for affection when he wants it, but not all the time. He doesn't have to share everything or go everywhere with you. He has his own life, thank you very much. He will share moments of affection, rather than hours of it.

62.

*Be kind to children just
as cats are kind to kittens*

Cats sometimes nurse another cat's kittens
or do babysitting duties. And even big,
bold tom cats often let kittens eat first.

63.

Enjoy partying, but not to excess

———

Your cat may enjoy the occasional night on the tiles, but she also likes the deep peace of a large bed. She knows that too many wild nights are not good for her.

64.

Steer clear of harassment

Cats dislike being harassed for affection and wisely walk away. Stay away from people who pester you with unwanted affection, offensive remarks or sexual advances. Guard your boundaries from invasion by others.

65.

Let go of your adult children

Caring cats encourage their grown-up kittens to be independent and leave the nest. They teach them what they need in life and then without regret they let each kitten go out into a wider world.

66.

You always have a choice

Cats choose whether to obey their humans. Sometimes they do. If it suits them. Sometimes they don't. If it suits them. *Unthinking* obedience or unthinking disobedience have no part in a sensible life.

67.

Avoid unpredictable or inconsistent people whenever possible

——

You don't need them in your life. Nor do cats.

68.

*Cats don't do guilt
or shame, so why
should you?*

———

Apologise if necessary and then just
move on.

69.

Make other people's guilt work in your favour

Cats do that very well indeed. They meow pitifully for food. They purr loudly to wake you up even on Sunday mornings. And cats that have decided they need a new home will sit outside your front door looking pathetic.

70.

Avoid controlling people, if you can

———

Cats do not submit to control. It's no fun to be around people that always know best, lay down the law, give unwanted advice or tell you what to do. Your cat likes the freedom to go his own way. You have the right to be as free as your cat.

71.

Do not try to control others

Stop telling other people what to do or demanding that they do it your way. Cats do not issue orders. Accept others as they are, not as you would like them to be.

Feline Ways to Care for Yourself

72.

Vanity is a human not a feline weakness

———

Your cat lives without vanity. In its place he has a proper appreciation for his own inner worth and outer grace. There *is* a difference.

73.

Take cleanliness seriously

——

Like cats, groom yourself every day from the tip of your nose to the soles of your feet.

74.

Be as fit as a feline

—

Running and jumping are two of the joys of life. Your cat can jump about six times his body length. You will never be able to jump up onto the top of the garden fence like your cat, but you can jog, work out, walk, weight train, cycle or swim!

75.
Don't risk a bad hair day

Wash and groom your hair regularly.
Your cat does.

76.

Cultivate gracefulness

___

Watch your cat leaping, twisting in the air, stalking, or just placing one silent foot after another. Graceful movements come naturally to cats, but can be learned by humans. Dancing, skating, yoga, pilates and gymnastics all help the body move gracefully.

77.

Stre . . . e . . . etch

Stretching before and after exercise, or almost any time, is good for the body. Adopt your cat's stretching regime.

78.

Motivate yourself into a healthy routine

———

Routines sound boring, but cats thrive
on settled routines. Make sure you have
good routines for eating, exercise and
sleeping – and thrive like your cat.

79.

Learn to enjoy being alone

Cats don't *need* company to have a good time. Cultivate self-reliance and enjoy your own company.

80.

Don't stick around in an abusive household

If people are threatening or hurting you, leave home. If in doubt, get out. That's what a cat would do.

Feline Ways to Relax and Rest

81.

Relax

———

Just take a look at your cat. Have you ever seen a more relaxed being? Cats epitomise the art of sublime relaxation.

82.

Slow down

Stop being a human doing and become a
human being. Cats don't feel the need
for constant busyness. They have learned
how to be, as well as how to do. No cat
does too much: they just are.

83.

Invest in a good bed

—

Cats and humans spend a lot of their life in bed. A bed should be soft and warm, out of draughts, and always inviting. If you are lucky, your generous cat will allow you enough space on your own bed.

84.

Share the warmth

———

Your cat is like a free hot water bottle for
you. You are like a large hot water bottle
for her. It is good to share warmth with
somebody you love.

85.

Sleep well and sleep long

———

Your cat never suffers from insomnia.
Cats sleep everywhere – on the bed, sofa,
top of the wardrobe, carpet, table, lap,
armchair, flowerbed, tree stump, on the
keyboard, in any cardboard box. Your cat
doesn't stay up late watching box sets or
late-night TV.

86.

Unwind with a daytime nap

Your cat knows the value of a quick snooze at any time. After a power nap, you will feel refreshed and ready to go. Down time is important for both cats and humans.

87.

Sunlight is good for cats and humans

Your cat never misses a chance to lie in the sunlight. Get out into the sunlight whenever possible.

88.

Find a warm place

An open fire or a hot stove make a focus of luxurious comfort in any room. Your cat loves sitting in front of a fire or a burning stove. Radiators are great, but a roaring fire is even better on a cold winter night. Settle down and enjoy it with her.

89.

Learn the art of doing nothing very much

———

Nothing in particular . . . or even nothing at all. Cats know when simply to laze and loll about.

Feline Ways to
Be a Cool Cat

90.

Cats are the epitome of cool

———

They have emotions too, but they conceal them from outsiders. Why give up their feline poise? Maintain an air of composure and keep others guessing.

91.

Cultivate the gift of serenity

———

As they sit and purr, cats are an example of serenity to us all. Take slow, deep breaths. Banish those negative thoughts and attitudes that distress you. Think about something happy and calm.

92.

Remain curious

——

Cats are interested in everything that goes on around them. They watch and investigate anything new. Asking questions – in the office, at home, before a purchase – is never a waste of time.

93.

Trust your instincts

If your instinct is telling you something is not as it should be, pay attention to that warning. If you feel fear, don't ignore the feeling. When cats are frightened, they proceed with caution. They don't pretend to be brave. They don't take unnecessary risks.

94.

Don't let jealousy ruin romance

——

Cats don't. There may be a lot of feline caterwauling, but there is rarely serious rivalry. They are not possessive about their mates.

95.

Be cool about social media

Some cats have millions of followers on social media, but they don't care a whisker about them. They don't want to be a celebrity, because they know every cat is *already* a celebrity. They don't bother to read the YouTube comments or track the ratings. They don't count the 'likes' or agonise over the number of friends or followers on Facebook, Twitter or Instagram. And they never, *ever*, Google their name to see what is written about them.

96.

Envying others leads to unhappiness

Your cat doesn't envy cats that have a better pedigree, live in a larger house or have a longer, bushier tail. She doesn't compare herself with the next-door cat. She knows that comparisons are always odious.

97.

Family is important to humans and cats

Cats that have grown up together as kittens usually stay friends for life. That early bond is rarely if ever broken. Stay with and play with family.

98.

Stay away from people you hate

––––––

That's what cats do. They don't sit around in the company of people they loathe, suffering in a state of simmering resentment. They practise positive avoidance.

99.

Contentment can be learned

Nothing in life is purrfect, but much of life is good enough. You may not get everything you like, but you can like everything you get. Cats are good at finding out the good things of life, whether it's a patch of sunlight or a soft pile of clean laundry to sleep on. Look for the little things that make you happy, like petting your cat.

100.

Tread softly and lightly over the world

Don't trample upon other people's hopes and dreams, but leave light footprints on their hearts.

Like your cat.

Visit Celia Haddon's website
www.celiahaddon.com
for useful advice about cats and other
small animals.

She can be found on Facebook at
www.facebook.com/CeliaHaddonBooks

Her cat, George, blogs at
george-online.blogspot.co.uk